Dream

BIG

Wyatt & Sons Publishers books may be ordered through booksellers or by contacting:

Wyatt & Sons Publishers, LLC
Mobile, Alabama 36695
www.wyattpublishing.com
editor@wyattpublishing.com

Because of the dynamic nature of the Internet, any web address or links contained in this book may have changed since publication and may no longer be valid.

Cover illustrations by: Cobi Tracy
Cover design by: Mark Wyatt
Interior design by: Mark Wyatt
ISBN 13:978-1-954798-30-4
Printed in the United States of America

This book was created by the Institute for Disability Studies through its Transition of Teens to Adult Life (ToTAL) program, which is funded through a contract with the Mississippi Department of Rehabilitation Services.

INSTITUTE FOR DISABILITY STUDIES
THE UNIVERSITY OF SOUTHERN MISSISSIPPI

Dream BIG

Written and Illustrated by
Gulfport High School Self-Advocates

W&S

WYATT & SONS
PUBLISHERS, LLC
Mobile, Alabama

Cambree's Perfect Day
By Cambree Durr

The perfect day that makes me the happiest is going to school and being with my friends. I would go to Sonic for food, and I would go with Damonta.

If I Had a Car
By Cambree Durr

If I had a car, I would never be at home.
The kind of car it would be is a Hellcat SRT.

My Future Career Goals
By Cambree Durr

I would rather work inside
because I don't want to have a heat stroke
while in the sun.
I would rather work with other people
because my job is required
to work with other people.

My Kind Perfect Friend
By Cambree Durr

The perfect friend to me
is someone who is kind.
I want a kind friend
because if they aren't kind
they can kick rocks.

Helping Hands
By Chris Brown

I would rather work inside
because I like cleaning up.
I would rather work with other people.

Red Fast Car
By Chris Brown

A charger, it go fast too.
I love fast cars.
Go to the park.
Basketball court, I love basketball.
My brother loves basketball.
He loves football too.
My car is red.
It is fast.

Perfect Day of Play
By Chris Brown

I go outside and go play. We go play basketball.
I go play with my friend. Play on my dad's phone.
We go get Wendy's.
I like Wendy's. It is good.
After Wendy's we go to my cousin's place.
We have fun in the house and play my papa's game.

Laser Tag Secret Door
By Chris Brown

If I found a secret door in my room, it would lead to
laser tag. They will tell us no running in there. We go to
the car place.

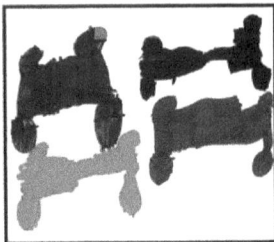

Reaching My Goals
By Damonta Byrd

Work outside
because fresh air.
I would rather work
with both my hands and mind.
People because to get the job done.

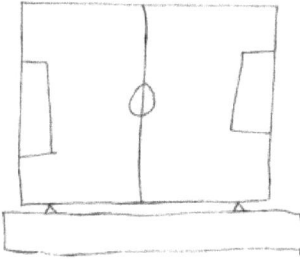

My Chill Perfect Friend
By Damonta Byrd

The perfect friend to me
is someone who is chill.
When a friend is chill,
it means someone who can vibe
and not do too much.

My Happiest Day
By Damonta Byrd

My happiest day
would be spending the day
with my friend Cambree in school.
I would go to Sonic to eat
and then return to school
to do my schoolwork.

My Dream Car
By Damonta Byrd

My dream car
is a Cyber truck.
Red,
and I will go to the race track with it
and after
show it to my mom.

Career Goals
By Darren Mahaffey

I want to work inside because it gets too hot outside.
I would work Alone.

A Friend Like Me
By Darren Mahaffey

The qualities I look for in a friend are to be cool,
hang out, and be kind, because I want that friend to
relate to me.

A Day with My Dad
By Darren Mahaffey
The perfect day for me would be if my dad was still
alive. My dad's name was Dwayne.
I would be happy because we would be able to do a lot
more stuff together.

A Goal of Mine
By Darren Mahaffey

When I get my license I will get a pickup truck.
I would drive around the neighborhood.
That I reached a goal of mine.

Teamwork
By Jakiryn Robinson

I would want to work inside.
I would want to work inside
because I will work harder.
Work with other people

A Circus Friend Like No Other
By Jakiryn Robinson

My perfect friend is kind, crazy, and she talks too
much. My friend likes to play games with me.

My Perfect Day
By Jakiryn Robinson

On my perfect day I would go
to my dad's home and watch TV.
I would also like to go outside and then play Fortnite.

My Car
By Jakiryn Robinson

I would have a Lamborghini.
I would drive to McDonalds.
I would feel happy.

Catnap
By Jakiryn Robinson

If I found a secret door, I would find Catnap.
We would have fun.
Go to McDonald, then have fun with DogDay
and Poppy.

Perfect Day's Adventure
By JaQuris Seymour

In my perfect day I would watch Madea's Halloween, Godzilla, and Chupacabra at my granny's house. I would go to my granny's house with my titi, cousins, papa, mom, and daddy Edward. I would love to go to Disney World and see Minnie and Mickey Mouse along with SpongeBob. I would enjoy going to see my friends and being able to say hello.

Driving Journey
By JaQuris Seymour

If I had a car, I would go to McDonald's and get a happy meal. I would have a huge truck and it would be fast.I would go to the pet store and see the hamsters, goldfish and snakes.

Kannita's Career Goals
By Kannita Mayers

I would rather work inside because I'm not trying to work in that hot heat and be sweating.
I would rather work with other people because I like working in groups and getting the job done.

My Perfect Honest friend
By Kannita Mayers

The perfect friend to me is someone that is honest with me because I don't want nobody lying to me.
I like honest friends to be my friends.

Perfect Day with My Cousin
By Kannita Mayers

My perfect day, that would make me the happiest is go by my cousin's house and go to get something to eat and we will make videos.

Driver's License

By Kannita Mayers

If I had a driver's license and a car,
I will go everywhere
and my car is going to be a Lamborghini
and how would it make me feel?
It will make me soooo happy.

My Career Goal
By Latrell Paige

I would rather work inside because outside is hot.
I would rather work alone because I don't want to
work with other people.

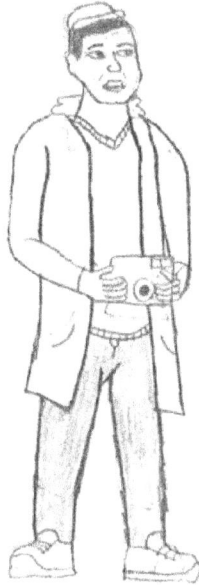

Perfect Friend
By Latrell Paige

My perfect friend is Trustworthy.

Win The Game
By Latrell Paige

I am happy because I win the video game I beat.

Dream Car
By Latrell Paige

The car is the jeep.

Swirl
By Marquese Johnson

Colorful Handprint
By Marshand Washington

Mia's Career Goals
By Mia Merrell

I would rather work outside, because it's better than work inside. I would work with other people.

Perfect Friend for Me
By Mia Merrell

The perfect friend for me is someone whose qualities are kind, honest, and sharing. Because otherwise, they wouldn't be so nice.

Day At the Mall
By Mia Merrell

My perfect day will be spending the day with my grand-parents at the mall. I will do shopping at the mall.

My Small Pink Car
By Mia Merrell

If I have small pink car,
I will drive to driving school.
I will feel great in a pink car.

My Future Career
By Roger Cunningham

I would rather work outside
because I like to be outside.
I would rather work with other people
because my job going to get done faster.

The Honest Perfect Friend
By Roger Cunningham

The perfect friend to me is someone who is honest
because no one want no friend who going to lie to me.

A Family Day
By Roger Cunningham

The perfect day would make me the happiest
I would stay home and play the game with my bruddas.

If I Had a Driver's License
By Roger Cunningham

If I had my driver license I would have a BMW.
I would probably go out of state
and I would feel happy.

Sara's Career Goals
By Sara Fairley
I would rather work outside because I like the sun.
I would rather work alone.

My Perfect Happy Friend
By Sara Fairley

My perfect friend is happy, a friend, and likes to play at
the playground. My friend likes to do his homework.

Sara's Perfect Day
By Sara Fairley

On my perfect day,
I would go to a restaurant
and eat barbecued Pepper.
I would like to go with my dad.

Pink Dream Car
By Sara Fairley

I would like to go
to a barbecued pepper restaurant
with my dad.
Ride by bank
happy
pink
slow.

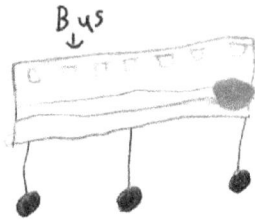

A Perfect friend
By Bernard Hanshaw

Kind
Honest
Helpful
Listens
Good friend

A Day to Make Me Smile
By Bernard Hanshaw

In my perfect day what would make me smile is
my girlfriend and Baseball.

My Yellow Van
By Bernard Hanshaw

My dream car is Van Yellow. I would drive to the mall.
Having my dream car would make me feel happy.

My YouTube Career Goals

By Dereianna Bowie

I would like to work inside because I'm thinking inside would be better for me.

I would like alone because it would be better. If I work with people I would get mad and frustrated too quick. I would work with my mind because when I become a YouTuber I got to think about ideas.

I want to work during the day because it will be more productive for me. I want to work for myself. I will make money for myself.

I would like to be a YouTuber.

My Perfect Trustworthy Friend

By Dereianna Bowie

The perfect friend to me is someone who is honest. I want a trustworthy friend because I would want to trust them no matter what.

My Perfect Day
By Dereianna Bowie

The perfect day will be nice hanging with my niece.
We would go to the park.

Bora Bora
By Dereianna Bowie

I would go hang out with my friends in my dream car
Lamborghini and go to the airport and fly to Bora Bora.

Teamwork in the Sun
By Edward Thompson

I like to work outside because of the sun!
I like to work with other people because you can meet
new people. I would like to work using my hands doing
construction.
I want to work during the day because I will be more
productive. I want to work by myself to earn money.

Super McDonald's Speed Runner
By Edward Thompson

The way I will use my power is by being a server at McDonald's.
A day at McDonald's will look like a flash because my fast runner power will help me to do things faster. Something that will be easy is that chores will be done in time. Something is difficult is that I could trip or spill things.

Secret Door to the Mall
By Edward Thompson

My secret door will lead to the mall
It will have a lot of food and tv's and arcade.
It will have free tokens and GameStop free game.

Perfect Gaming Day
By Edward Thompson

My perfect day that makes me happiest is going out to eat and playing the game with my friends and draw.

Perfect Friend

Edward's Dream Car
By Edward Thompson

My imagine dream car is Lamborghini.
It will make me feel good.

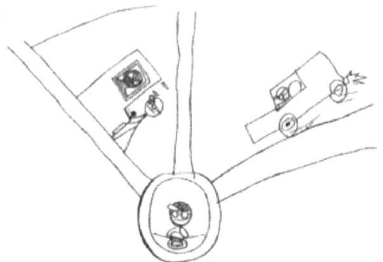

Bacon World
By Edward Thompson

My candy world will be full with bacon.
My house will be bacon.
The fish will be gummy.

My Wal-Mart Career Goals
By Izaiah Sams

I work for inside.
Work with other people.
Work with rough hands.
Work at night.
Work for self.
Wal-Mart.

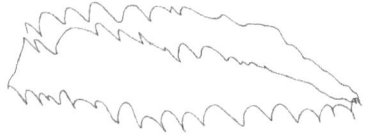

Wal-Mart
By Izaiah Sams

Job Wal-Mart. That is a good job.

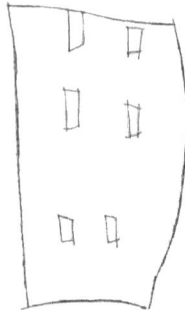

Dog So Cute
By Izaiah Sams

The dog so cute and isn't the dog so cool? I love the snack cart. I love the cart so cool. Reeses look so good.

So Cool
By Izaiah Sams

Funny the friend, it is so cool.
I love my mom.I love my dad.
I love my sister it is so cool.
I love my broth so cool.
My lil broth so cool.

Rmt mon
ant dad

My Choice To Be Me
By Izaiah Sams

If I was a character in any video game,
I would be myself.
I want to be myself because that's my choice.

Jordan's Career Goals
By Jordan Johnson

I would rather work in a building, building with a team.
I would rather work with my mind yes.
I would rather work at night.
I want to work for a boss because
I don't want to be fired.

Perfect Friend to Others
By Jordan Johnson

The perfect friend to others.
Kind, Funny, Honest
Sharing, Helpful
Plays fair
Listens, Trustworthy, Forgiving
Fun to love

Hallcat
By Jordan Johnson

Hallcat. Fast car Red hallcat. fast.

Space Drums
By Jordan Johnson

My favorite hobby is playing on the drums.
I would play the drums in space for my alien friends.
I would play the drums and it will turn everyone into animals.
The sky would be gray and my friends would fall from the sky. They all scream and cheer and fall down with pumpkin pie.
My friends are happy being on a farm.
My alien friends will walk amongst a calling storm.

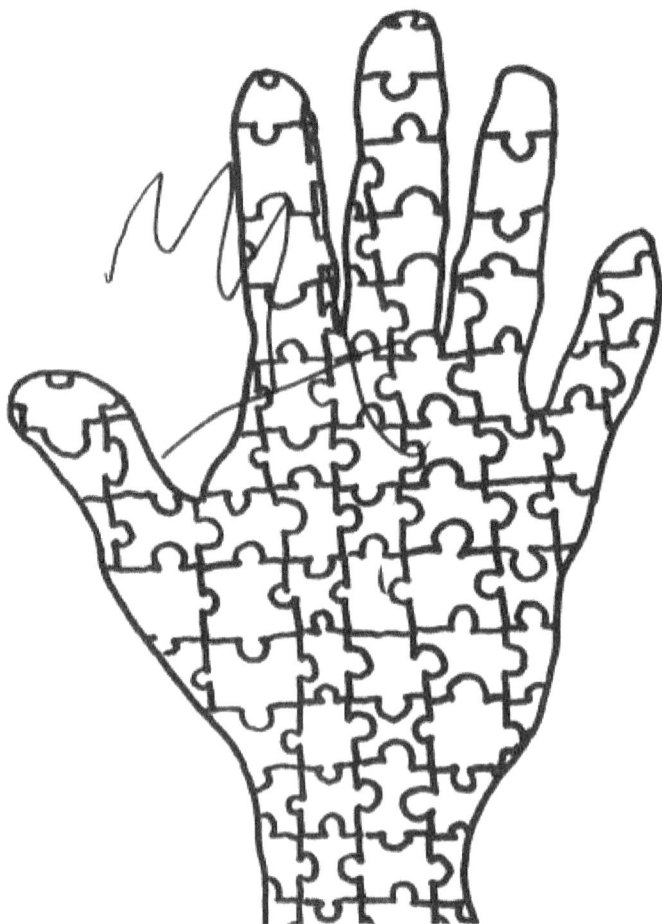

Max's Handprint
By Max Dunworth

Would you Rather
By Ozrreal Logan

I would rather work inside because it is cool inside.
I would rather work alone because I would focus more.
I would rather work with my hands because you can do
so much with your hands. I would rather work during
the day because I would work harder.
I would rather work for a boss because I would follow
directions.

Perfect Friend to Talk to
By Ozrreal Logan

The Perfect friend to me is someone who is honest
because I can trust them with anything and I can talk
to them about anything also they have no drama going
on.

Family Day at the Beach
By Ozrreal Logan

My Perfect day that would make me smile all day is
going to the beach with family and friends because I get
to hang out with them.

Purple Lamborghini
By Ozrreal Logan

My dream car is a Purple Lamborghini and I would drive it to Miami Florida and it would make me feel amazing.

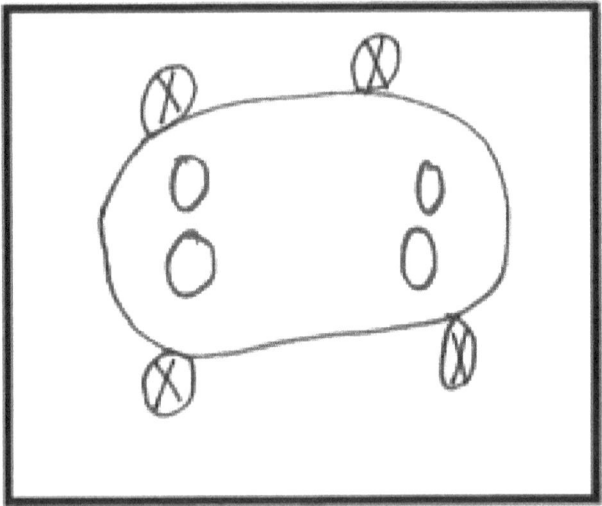

Super Supermodel
By Ozrreal Logan

I would design my dream job.
Mine is to be a model
Also if I were a superhero
I would be a runway model hero.
My power would be to help other people.
My hobby is to listen to music. Something fun I
would do is practice how to walk the runway.
My day in my job would look really fun.

Model

Gaming World

By Ozrreal Logan

If I discovered a secret door in my room it would be a gaming world. I would find a gaming character. We would play all kinds of different games.

Me Gaming world
Gaming character

World of candy

By Ozrreal Logan

If I woke up to a world being filled with candy everything would be made out of milk chocolate. I would try to eat all of it.

milk Chocolate world

Engineer
By Sam Miskell

I would like to work inside because of the cool air.
I would like to work using my mind because I want to
be an engineer. I would like to work for myself.

Sam's Dream Car
By Sam Miskell

My dream car is a Tesla.
I would drive my Tesla
to my house.
Having a Tesla would
make me feel good.

Beach Day
By Sam Miskell

Snakes
By Sam Miskell

44

Trevion's Career Goals
By Trevion Crandle

I like to work inside.
I like to work with other people because it's fun.
I like to work with my hands.
I like to work during the day.
Work for myself.

Personal Super Strength Trainer
By Trevion Crandle

The way I would combine my super strength with my dream job at the gym is by lifting as many weights as possible. My day will start by helping someone lift weights and get in shape. Something easy to do in my job with my superpowers will be picking up stuff. Something difficult will be that because of my super strength I can break stuff.

My Secret WWE Door
By Trevion Crandle

My secret door is to a WWE game.
In face in a match, Roman Reigns and he tried to cheat.
I got back up and I won.

The Perfect Funny Friend
By Trevion Crandle

The perfect friend to me is someone who is funny.

Trevion's Perfect Day
By Trevion Crandle

The perfect day is have a car and a home.

Dream Cars
By Trevion Triplett

I need a Lamborghini
Bugatti
Charger
Mustang
Tesla
Big body Chevrolet

The Backrooms
By Trevion Triplett

The backrooms is an entities world
and is the most scary place in the universe.

Superpower Batman
By Trevion Triplett

My superpower is Batman.
I'm him. I'm a rich billionaire
and a YouTuber.

About the Authors

Bernard Hanshaw
Bernard is a sophomore at Gulfport High School. His favorite things to do are playing his Xbox and playing Mario Kart. His hobbies are playing football, basketball, and baseball. When he grows up, he wants to be a soccer player, a golfer, or a PlayStation gamer.

Cambree Durr
Cambree is a senior at Gulfport High School. She enjoys driving and listening to music, and she likes playing ROBLOX. When Cambree grows up, she wants to be a nurse. She has two cats named Sushi and Saki.

Christopher Brown
Chris is a sophomore and his favorite thing to do is ride his bike. He has two pets, and their names are Emoji and Rosie. His hobbies are playing video games, hanging out outside, and cleaning. When Chris grows up, he wants to be an Uber driver.

Damonta Byrd
Damonta was born in Atlanta. He has two pets. Their names are Chicago and Snake. His favorite thing to do is play basketball. When Damonta grows up, he wants to be a basketball player.

Darren Mahaffey
Darren's favorite animal is a cat. Darren likes working on cars. He also enjoys playing and watching football, and he wants to be a football player when he grows up.

Dereianna Bowie
Dereianna is a junior in high school. She likes dancing and playing with her BFF as well as listening to music, doing hair, and playing volleyball. She wants to be a nurse or caretaker when she grows up.

Edward Thompson
Edward is a senior at Gulfport High School. He likes basketball and football, but he also likes playing video games. He wants to be a gamer when he grows up. His favorite animal is the turtle.

Izaiah Sams
Izaiah is a sophomore in high school. His hobbies are playing baseball and jumping on the trampoline. His favorite animal is a tiger. His favorite thing to do is go outside. When Izaiah grows up, he wants to become a doctor.

JaQuris Seymour
JaQuris is a high school graduate of 2024. His hobbies are playing basketball and watching animals. He has a dog named Tia and his favorite thing to do is watch movies.

Jakyrin Robinson
Jakyrin is a student at Gulfport High School. His favorite thing to do is to relax and watch TV. When he grows up, he wants to be in the movies.

Jordan Johnson
Jordan is a sophomore at Gulfport High School. He enjoys sleeping and napping and playing video games. Jordan wants to be an officer when he grows up. His favorite animal is the iguana.

Kannita Mayers
Kannita was born in Gulfport, Mississippi. Her favorite thing to do is dance. When Kannita grows up, she wants to be a hair stylist.

Latrell Paige
Latrell is a senior at Gulfport High School. He likes playing video games, cleaning up, and fishing. When he grows up, he wants to be on the night watch. His favorite animal is the Pitbull.

Marshand Washington
Marshand was born in Stone Mountain, Georgia. His favorite things to do are sing and dance. When Marshand grows up, he wants to be as independent as he can be.

Marquese Johnson

Marquese was born in Cape Girardeau, Missouri. His favorite thing to do is toss and throw things into the air. When Marquese grows up, he wants to be as independent as he can be.

Max Dunworth

Max Dunworth is a senior in high school. His hobbies are playing buddy ball baseball, going to the library, and walking. He also has a dog named Ruby. His favorite thing to do is going to eat and getting burritos. When Max grows up, he wants to be a baseball player.

Mia Merrell

Mia is a sophomore at Gulfport High School. She likes playing Pokémon games and drawing and her favorite animal is the fox. When she grows up, she wants to be a traveler.

Ozrreal Logan

Ozrreal is a senior at Gulfport High School. She likes singing, jamming to music, and playing video games. She wants to be a model when she grows up. Her favorite animal is the zebra.

Roger Cunningham

Roger is a senior at Gulfport High School. He likes playing football and GTA 5, sleeping, and helping folks. When he grows up, he wants to work at a zoo.

Sam Miskell

Sam is a junior at Gulfport High School. He likes to play video games, football, basketball, and soccer. When he grows up, he wants to be a mechanic, driver, and work in customer service.

Sara Fairley

Sara is a senior at Gulfport High School. She likes going to the beach and going fishing, as well as watching YouTube videos. She wants to be a police officer when she grows up. Her favorite animals are cats and pigs.

Trevion Crandle

Trevion's favorite animals are dogs. His hobbies are cleaning and going outside and his favorite thing to do is watch Twitch. When Trevion grows up, he wants to be either a busser or a personal trainer.

Trevion Triplett

Trevion is currently a junior. His hobbies are playing video games and watching anime. His favorite animal is a dog. His favorite thing to do is make YouTube videos. When Trevion grows up, he wants to be a therapist and a YouTuber.